P9-DMV-603

Saylor Baldwin Kincaid

2017

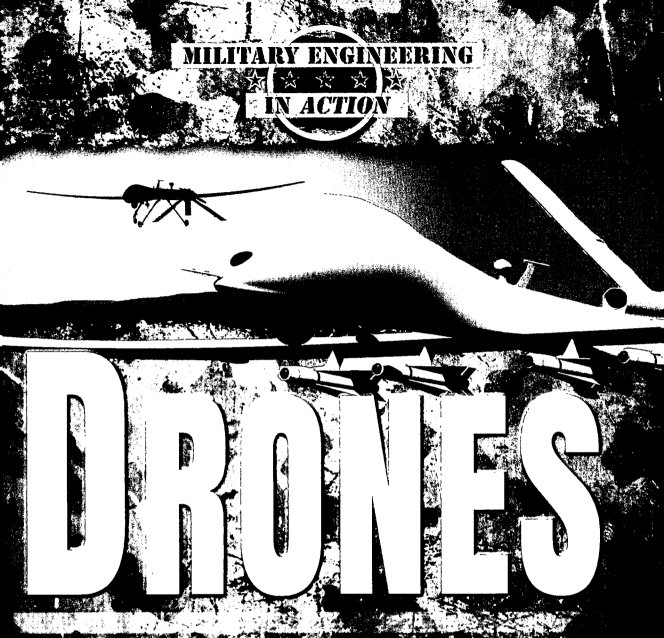

MILITARY ENGINEERING
IN ACTION

DRONES

REMOTE-CONTROLLED WARFARE

Judy Silverstein Gray and Taylor Baldwin Kiland

Enslow Publishing
101 W. 23rd Street
Suite 240
New York, NY 10011
USA

enslow.com

Acknowledgments

A very special thank you to Jackson Edward Kiland for your insight, wisdom, and enthusiasm—we loved your perspective! Another special thank you goes to Rich Gray, whose eagle eye, meticulous read, and curiosity kept us sharp.

Published in 2017 by Enslow Publishing, LLC.
101 W. 23rd Street, Suite 240, New York, NY 10011

Library of Congress Cataloging-in-Publication Data

Names: Gray, Judy Silverstein, author. | Kiland, Taylor Baldwin, 1966- author.
Title: Drones : remote-controlled warfare / Judy Silverstein Gray and Taylor Baldwin Kiland.
Description: New York, NY : Enslow Publishing, [2017] | Series: Military engineering in action | Includes
  bibliographical references and index.
Identifiers: LCCN 2016012432| ISBN 9780766075122 (library bound) | ISBN 9780766075108 (pbk.) | ISBN
  9780766075115 (6-pack)
Subjects: LCSH: Drone aircraft—Juvenile literature. | Air pilots, Military—United States—Juvenile literature.
Classification: LCC UG1242.D7 G72 2016 | DDC 623.74/69—dc23
LC record available at http://lccn.loc.gov/2016012432

Printed in the United States of America

To Our Readers: We have done our best to make sure all website addresses in this book were active and appropriate when we went to press. However, the author and the publisher have no control over and assume no liability for the material available on those websites or on any websites they may link to. Any comments or suggestions can be sent by e-mail to customerservice@enslow.com.

Photos Credits: Cover, p. 1 iStock.com/biosdi (drone at sunset), Paul Fleet/Shutterstock.com (drone in foreground); art/background throughout Dianka Pyzhova/Shutterstock.com, Ensuper/Shutterstock.com, foxie/Shutterstock.com, kasha_malasha/Shutterstock.com, pashabop/Shutterstock.com; p. 2 Dejan Lazarevic/Shutterstock.com; p. 5 U.S. Navy/Mass Communication Specialist 1st Class Peter D. Lawlor; p. 6 U.S. Air Force/Lt Col Leslie Pratt; p. 7 U.S. Air Force/Senior Master Sgt. C.R.; p. 9 US Air Force; p. 12 Apic/Getty Images; p. 14 US Air Force/WikimediaCommons/Kettering-bug-1.jpg/Public Domain, Greg5030/WikimediaCommons/KetteringAerialTorpedo.jpg/Creative Commons Attribution-Share Alike 3.0 Unported; p. 17 Usmc/Getty Images; p. 18 Time Life Pictures/US Army/The LIFE Picture Collection/Getty Images; p. 21 U.S. Air Force photo/Staff Sgt. Vernon Young Jr.; p. 23 Bret Hartman/The Washington Post/Getty Images; pp. 25, 26 Getty Images News/Getty Images; pp. 28, 38 Ethan Miller/Getty Images; p. 32 Isaac Brekken/Getty Images; p. 33 Andreas Rentz/Getty Images; p. 34 The Asahi Shimbun/Getty Images; p. 37 John Moore/Getty Images; p. 42 U.S. Navy/Mass Communication Specialist 3rd Class Edward Guttierez III; p. 43 Jose CABEZAS/AFP/GettyImages.

CONTENTS

CHAPTER 1 — Capturing the Captain From Thousands of Miles Away 4

CHAPTER 2 — The History and Technology Evolution of Unmanned Flight 11

CHAPTER 3 — The Predator: From an Eye in the Sky to a Futuristic Weapon 20

CHAPTER 4 — A Day in the Life of a Drone Pilot 31

CHAPTER 5 — So You Want to Be a Drone Pilot? . . . 36

CHAPTER 6 — The Future 40

Timeline 45

Glossary 46

Further Reading 47

Index 48

CHAPTER 1

Capturing the Captain From Thousands of Miles Away

After US Air Force Lieutenant Colonel T. Mark McCurley had tracked his target—the Captain—for sixty days, McCurley could predict his location by the minute. The Captain's behavior followed a routine and became predictable. It made McCurley's job of tailing the Captain so much easier.

The Captain was a nickname McCurley and his crew at Nellis Air Force Base outside Las Vegas, Nevada, had given to a terrorist within the Al Qaeda terrorist network. This organization was led by Osama bin Laden, the man who coordinated the September 11, 2001, attacks on the United States. The Captain was part of bin Laden's inner circle of terrorist advisors. US intelligence experts believed

A Predator C Avenger is an unmanned aerial vehicle.

he was responsible for the 2001 deaths of Americans. As McCurley said in his book *Hunter Killer: Inside America's Unmanned Air War*, "If Osama bin Laden was the head of the snake, the Captain was the fangs."

McCurley was part of a secretive counterterrorism program using drones, or unmanned aircraft, to hunt terrorists from the sky. A drone pilot, he was trained to remotely fly these aircraft from a secret trailer at Nellis Air Force Base. Thousands of miles from the mountain camps of northeast Afghanistan and Pakistan, McCurley tracked the enemy.

The MQ-1 Predator unmanned aircraft is a set of eyes in the sky. Notice the black missile attached to the underside of the drone.

The aircraft, called the Predator, is small, quiet, and able to fly at altitudes of up to twenty-five thousand feet and at ranges up to 675 miles (1,086 kilometers). It can trail a target virtually undetected. And that's what McCurley had been doing for two months. Day after day, he had watched as the Captain left his home early in the morning on the back of a motorcycle. He was driven over dusty roads to daily meetings with other terrorists and messengers. He traveled the same route, making the same stops nearly every day. He did not return home until well after midnight most evenings. As McCurley said in *Hunter Killer*, "We knew his every move." Now it

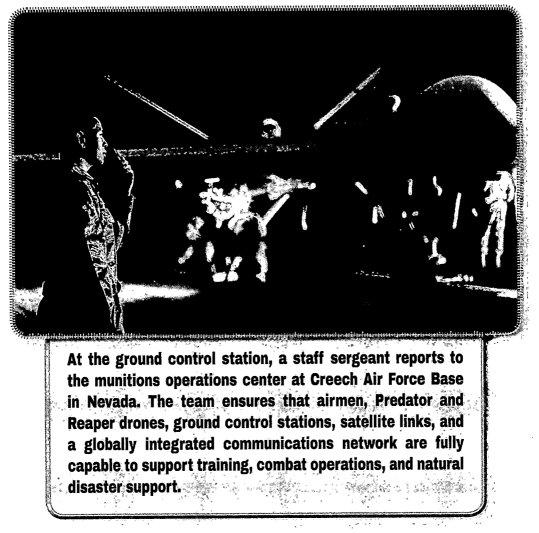

At the ground control station, a staff sergeant reports to the munitions operations center at Creech Air Force Base in Nevada. The team ensures that airmen, Predator and Reaper drones, ground control stations, satellite links, and a globally integrated communications network are fully capable to support training, combat operations, and natural disaster support.

was time to use this information. McCurley's drone from the sky and the special operations team on the ground were going to capture the Captain with precise information provided by the drone.

On the appointed day, McCurley remembers, "I could feel a tingle of excitement shoot through my body . . . I knew the village. It was seared into my mental map, since I'd flown over it for weeks now." Or, more accurately, his Predator drone had flown over the village for weeks.

FACT

Drone Sorties and Strikes

By 2015, almost 2,500 people had been killed by drone-launched missile strikes, according to the Bureau of Investigative Journalism. The military conducts about sixty drone sorties, or missions, each day, and the US Air Force says it needs to train three hundred new drone pilots annually. According to a *Military Times* report from August 2015, that will help the military keep up with the demand for drone missions, given worldwide events.

It was McCurley's job once again to track the Captain on his daily rounds. The ground team set up an observation point on his route in a remote area between two villages. To provide backup support, they stationed a second team dressed as locals traveling along the road. The Captain and his driver sped past and McCurley reported: "Target has passed first checkpoint."

The second team then blocked the passage so the Captain couldn't turn around and escape. The first team lay in wait in a graveyard up ahead, dressed in full black burqas—the head-to-toe shrouds many women wear in Muslim countries. The team looked like a group of mourners visiting a grave.

There was radio silence as everyone waited for the Captain to approach the ambush site. "When he got close, I watched as the team rushed out from the graveyard and surrounded the bike. They had their pistols and sub-machine guns drawn. The Captain's driver turned and attempted to flee."

How Are Drones Operated?

Drones are remotely controlled by a crew of two people, on the ground miles away. Instead of a cockpit, drones have a satellite dish. Connected to the aircraft by a satellite link, crew members sit in a small building in front of a group of computer screens. One of the crew members is called the sensor operator and is responsible for manipulating a turret under the drone's chin, which houses two video cameras. One camera shoots color video in daylight hours, and the other camera produces infrared images at night. The other crew member navigates the flight path of the drone.

Senior airmen fly an MQ-1 Predator.

While the action unfolded halfway across the world, McCurley watched intently on his computer. Using his camera's magnification from across the globe, he saw the backup team running toward the bike. "From more than twenty thousand feet, it looked like a baseball rundown."

Fleeing on foot, across a field and into a small, one-story mud house, the Captain kept McCurley and his Predator busy. The drone's cameras provided visual confirmation of the Captain's exact location to the ground teams, who were able to quickly surround the house and toss a tear gas canister inside. "Gas started to billow out of the door and the windows. Seconds later, the Captain stumbled out and surrendered."

A dangerous terrorist was now in US custody. According to intelligence experts, he later provided important information to his interrogators about other terrorists and future targets, thus thwarting future attacks.

McCurley turned off his computer, walked outside, got into his car, and drove home to the suburbs of Las Vegas, listening to news of the Captain's capture on his car radio. "When I heard the report, I had to smile." It was another victory for drones in the war on terrorism.

CHAPTER 2

The History and Technology Evolution of Unmanned Flight

ilitary forces have always sought new ways to see the ground from above and to visualize the entire battlefield from a distance. Almost a full century before the Wright brothers made their first powered flight in Kitty Hawk, North Carolina, the first unmanned aerial device—or drone—was used by the Royal Navy during the Napoleonic Wars. In 1806, Lord Thomas Cochrane, who earned the nickname Sea Wolf, was known for terrorizing the French coast. He seized enemy ships and captured their coastal military bases. To further assert his might and intimidate the population, he launched kites from his thirty-two-gun frigate, the HMS *Pallas*. The

The first flight of Orville Wright took place at Kill Devil Hills, Kitty Hawk, North Carolina, on December 17, 1903. His brother, Wilbur Wright, stands to the right. Almost one hundred years earlier, the first drone flew during the Napoleonic Wars.

kites' strings were lit on fire, and when the strings burned through, leaflets floated to the ground. The propaganda leaflets, written in French and making proclamations against Napoleon, were air dropped and terrified the local population.

In 1848, the Austrians decided to launch the first air raid in history—with balloons! Carefully calculating the proper wind currents, they launched two hundred balloons over the city of Venice (now part of Italy) armed with bombs that were controlled by timed fuses. But the tactic had mixed results: when the winds changed, some of the balloons ended up back in Austrian territory.

Perley's Balloons: Civil War "Drones"

The problem created by wind currents was addressed during the Civil War when New Yorker Charles Perley invented his version of an unmanned aerial bomber in 1863. It was really a hot air balloon with a special timing device. Perley also recommended using test balloons to gauge the direction of the wind before sending up the entire balloon force. His design included a hanging basket full of bombs attached to a timer. When the balloon was sent over enemy lines, the timer would trip a hinge that would open the basket and ignite the explosive. The bombs would then drop on the enemy and explode. Both Confederate and Union forces are said to have launched Perley's balloons, but with limited success.

The Flying Bombs of World War I

On the eve of the United States' entry into World War I in 1913, the first radio-controlled drone was developed. Dr. Peter Hewitt and Elmer A. Sperry used an automatic gyroscopic stabilizer to convert a US Navy Curtiss N-9 trainer aircraft. They called it the Hewitt-Sperry Automatic Airplane, or flying bomb. Launched by a catapult, it was able to fly fifty miles (80 km) carrying a three-hundred-pound (136-kilogram) bomb in several test flights.

Their invention never saw combat, but it did lead to another advancement in drone technology: the rail-launched Kettering Bug. Developed by the Dayton-Wright Airplane Company, it was a type of aerial torpedo, unmanned and guided by a preset timer. At a certain range, the timer would shut off the engine, the wings would be released, and the Bug would fall to the ground and detonate.

Despite some initial testing success, the Kettering Bug was never used in combat because officials worried about its reliability when carrying explosives over Allied troops.

A reproduction of the Kettering Bug is on display at the National Museum of the United States Air Force in Dayton, Ohio.

One problem with many of the early drones was that they could be used only once. There was no way to retrieve them! The Royal Navy and the Royal Air Force designed a radio-controlled drone in 1935 made of spruce and plywood. It was the first reusable drone. Called the Queen Bee, it was able to fly at altitudes of seventeen thousand feet (5,181 m) and at a maximum distance of three hundred miles (483 km). They were primarily used as target practice.

The Glide Bombs of World War II

During World War II, the United States and its allies developed and tested a variety of drones with mixed success. One of the most ambitious projects was Operation Aphrodite, using B-17s and B-24s filled with explosives. The planes were initially piloted by a two-man crew that would abandon the plane at two thousand feet (610 m)

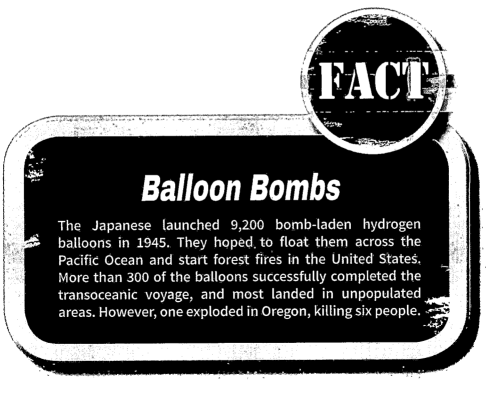

Balloon Bombs

The Japanese launched 9,200 bomb-laden hydrogen balloons in 1945. They hoped to float them across the Pacific Ocean and start forest fires in the United States. More than 300 of the balloons successfully completed the transoceanic voyage, and most landed in unpopulated areas. However, one exploded in Oregon, killing six people.

FACT

The First Aerial Images

Drones were first used to collect aerial images of the enemy during the Spanish-American War. In 1898, an American soldier named Corporal William Eddy attached a camera with a long shutter release to a kite. The photos he took were the first wartime surveillance photos in history, providing important information on enemy positions. Mounted on manned aircraft, aerial surveillance was first used extensively as a combat tool during World War I. The camera was mounted on an unmanned aircraft, as no reliable remote control technology existed.

in altitude. Before ejection, the pilots would set it on a course to destroy V-1 flying bomb launch sites. Remote operators would use a live feed from a television camera on board the abandoned planes to guide the flying bombs to their targets.

UAVs in the Cold War and Vietnam

When American Gary Powers was shot down in his U-2 spy plane over Russia in 1960, the Central Intelligence Agency (CIA) went to work on a new unmanned aerial vehicle (UAV) that could give the United States an advantage over the Soviet Union. It would also be safer since human pilots were not used. The US Air Force developed a combat UAV called the AQM-34 Ryan Firebee. It was air-launched from a DC-130 aircraft, dropped with a parachute, and recovered by a helicopter. The early models could remain in flight for two hours. Later, Ryan developed jet-propelled Firebees called Lightning Bugs. Providing secret surveillance from 1964–1975, they flew thirty-four thousand missions over Southeast Asia, North Korea, Cuba, and China.

Drones and Video Surveillance

In 1995, defense contractor General Atomics designed a remotely piloted glider carrying video cameras, which were relatively new to battle. Initially called the Gnat and renamed the RQ-1 Predator,

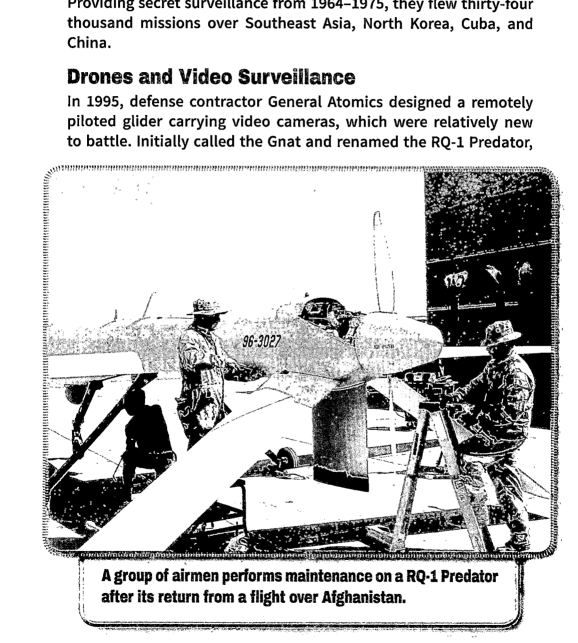

A group of airmen performs maintenance on a RQ-1 Predator after its return from a flight over Afghanistan.

What Is a Hellfire Missile?

Officially called the heliborne-launched fire-and-forget missile, the Hellfire is an air-to-surface weapon.
Specifications:
Weight: 100–108 pounds (45–49 kg)
Length: 64 inches (162.5 centimeters)
Diameter: 7 inches (17.78 cm)
Engine: solid-fuel rocket

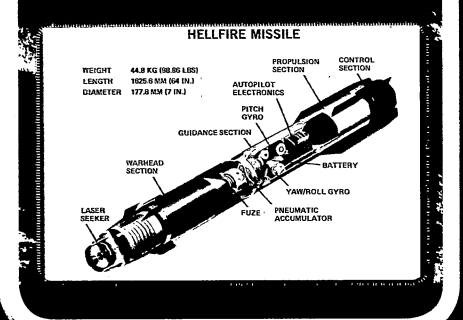

HELLFIRE MISSILE

WEIGHT	44.8 KG (98.86 LBS)
LENGTH	1625.6 MM (64 IN.)
DIAMETER	177.8 MM (7 IN.)

PROPULSION SECTION
CONTROL SECTION
AUTOPILOT ELECTRONICS
PITCH GYRO
GUIDANCE SECTION
WARHEAD SECTION
BATTERY
YAW/ROLL GYRO
LASER SEEKER
FUZE
PNEUMATIC ACCUMULATOR

it was capable of recording movement up to sixty miles (96 km) away, providing the big picture view that combat forces desired. It was eventually outfitted with Global Positioning System (GPS) navigation technology and used over Bosnia in 1994.

The Gnat had some limitations. It was vulnerable to bad weather and had a short range, requiring operators to be located nearby. This made it impossible for surveillance use against enemies in far-flung places across the world. Future models of the Predator solved many of these problems. The addition of a satellite communications data link, a deicing system, reinforced wings, and a laser-guided targeting system allowed use for precise surveillance. That paved the way for arming drones with modern weapons.

The Predator: From an Eye in the Sky to a Futuristic Weapon

Ｔhe Predator drone has a successor model, the MQ-9 Reaper. The Reaper is now the most common drone model used in the battle against global terrorism. Both of these drones had a humble beginning, starting with a young Israeli engineer with a big idea.

Abraham Karem had been fascinated with machines since childhood. He loved taking apart old radios to figure out how they worked. When he discovered the Aero Club of Israel as a teenager,

An MQ-1 Predator and its sucessor, the MQ-9 Reaper, are ready for their next mission.

he built his first glider and immediately became obsessed with designing aircraft.

Karem participated in many model glider competitions that aimed for endurance. The winning aircraft would be the one that maintained altitude for up to three and a half minutes. He became an international contestant in these competitions, winning tenth place at the free-flight glider World Championships in Austria in 1963, when he was twenty-six years old.

After finishing his education, Karem joined the Israeli Air Force and quickly earned a reputation as a problem solver. He led teams of designers that made fighter plane modifications for immediate use by the air force. Yet, after he was asked to design an unmanned decoy to deceive Soviet MIG fighter planes, he had an idea he wanted to pursue on his own. Karem wondered if a really smart decoy, capable of remaining in the sky for hours, could track enemy movements and launch missiles. He knew that being unmanned would reduce the decoy aircraft's weight, allowing it to stay in the air longer. He believed this type of aircraft could provide the 24/7 air defense that Israel needed in 1974. Convinced he would never be allowed to work at his own pace and on his own project ideas, he quit his job with the government and started his own company.

Having studied birds as design models for his gliders, Karem knew the albatross offered some traits he could imitate. Because its wingspan is twenty times wider than its length, it can glide over oceans for hours at a time. In aviation, this is known as a high aspect ratio wing.

In the book *Predator: The Secret Origins of the Drone Revolution*, author Richard Whittle discusses some of Karem's original thinking. Karem felt that previous drone designs were flawed since they were designed to fly for only a few hours at a time and because they were developed by engineers accustomed to building toys made with cheap, expendable materials. Karem was determined to design a model that could reliably stay airborne and survive in all kinds of weather conditions.

After several years of tinkering, he unveiled a prototype for the US military, successfully demonstrating that his design could practically defy the laws of gravity. Named the Albatross, his design weighed 105 pounds (47.6 kg) empty and 200 pounds (90.7 kg) when loaded with fuel. It could remain airborne for forty-eight hours on 15.2 gallons (57.5 liters) of gas. The plane's performance appealed to the US military.

Abraham Karem stands with the Albatross drone. Karem built the Albatross in his garage, and it led to the invention of the Predator drone used by military forces around the world.

Later, Karem sold his company to General Atomics, a defense contractor based in San Diego, California, where his design was renamed the Predator. He continued to perfect his design, and it caught the attention of the CIA in 1993, when the United States intervened to end the civil war among the Croatians, Serbians, and Muslim people in the Balkan region of Bosnia and Herzegovina.

In July 1994, Karem's design was tested over the wartime skies of the Bosnian capital of Sarajevo when it transmitted live video images back to ground control stations (GCS) in Italy and Germany. Although several drones were either shot down by ground forces or lost because of mechanical failure, no human lives were sacrificed. Additionally, each drone was one-tenth the cost of a jet fighter. Those benefits sparked the military's appetite for drones. Yet the Predator's full military potential wasn't realized until it was outfitted with weapons.

The Predator on the Hunt for bin Laden

In 1998, Muslim terrorists ran trucks with suicide bombs into the US embassies in Dar es Salaam, Tanzania, and Nairobi, Kenya. Those attacks killed 213 people and wounded more than 4,500. Taking credit, known terrorist Osama bin Laden and his Al Qaeda organization publicly announced their war on the United States in the name of Islam. While bin Laden had long been on the CIA's threat list, he was now in their crosshairs. It was a few years before Al Qaeda's infamous September 11, 2001, attacks on the World Trade Center and the Pentagon. Bin Laden was assassinated in 2011 but not until after his organization killed more than three thousand Americans in the 2001 attacks on American soil and after seven thousand service members died in combat in Iraq and Afghanistan. Finding bin Laden proved challenging, but surveillance drones offered the ideal capabilities for this mission.

The CIA had access to the technology and engineers of a secret unit within the air force nicknamed Big Safari. Officially called the 645th Aeronautical Systems Group at Wright-Patterson Air Force Base in Dayton, Ohio, the unit was created during the Cold War to help the CIA and the air force keep a watchful eye on the Soviet Union. They sought clever devices that could be rapidly purchased and deployed by both the military and the CIA to spy on its enemies.

Osama bin Laden is the terrorist who took credit for the September 11, 2001, terror attacks.

More than a decade after Predator surveillance confirmed his hideout in Afghanistan, Osama bin Laden was killed in this compound in Abbottabad, Pakistan, by US special forces.

Big Safari now looked to General Atomics to provide them with a Predator that could find bin Laden in the mountains of Afghanistan.

Within a month of deploying the Predator to bin Laden's presumed hideout in 2000, they located him on their seventh surveillance flight, as detailed by author Richard Whittle, in his book

Predator. The CIA had collected intelligence on the location of the village, the function of each of the town's buildings, and the exact times this particular village stopped its daily activities for prayer in a community building. After circling overhead for days, the Predator provided a clear video confirmation of the CIA's information. They watched as, just before noon, a "tall man in white robe," emerged from a mud and brick house to attend a midday prayer service. He was immediately surrounded by shorter men—some bowing to him and some guarding him. The video confirmed it was bin Laden. Yet without any weapon aboard the Predator, all the crew could do was to watch. Cruise missiles from a ship or submarine were too far away and would take too long to arrive on target—and the target might move. That could increase the chance of missing the target and killing civilians. The CIA knew it was time to arm the Predator with cruise missiles.

Armed With Hellfire Missiles

Big Safari and General Atomics searched for a weapon to use with the Predator, and they chose the Hellfire missile. A "smart" weapon, it could find its target by the light emitted from a laser. The Hellfire had proven its worth in the first Gulf War, when it was launched from helicopters, and the army had plenty. A new model of the Predator, called the Predator 3034, was modified to carry the missiles' extra weight.

According to Whittle, the newly armed Predator made its successful debut on October 7, 2001. It was just minutes after President George Bush announced that the United States was launching strikes in Afghanistan in retaliation for the September 11 attacks on US soil. In the middle of the night, in Afghanistan, the Predator 3034 (armed with two Hellfire missiles and code-named Wildfire 34), hovered above Kandahar. US forces were in hot pursuit of terrorist leader Mullah Mohammed Omar and his assistants. Wildfire's cameras transmitted video via a live satellite feed to the CIA and Pentagon, nearly seven thousand miles (11,265 km) away.

The Hellfire missile is attached to the underside of this MQ-1B Predator unmanned aircraft. In addition to carrying two laser-guided Hellfire missiles, the Predators have cameras that provide full-motion video.

General Atomics
MQ-1 Predator

Crew: 0 onboard, 2 in ground station

Length: 27 feet (8.2 m)

Height: 6.9 feet (2.1 m)

Wingspan: 48.7 feet (14.8 m)

Empty Weight: 1,130 lbs (512.5 kg)

Maximum Takeoff Weight: 2,250 lbs (1,020 kg)

Power Source: One Rotax 914F turbocharged four-cylinder engine

Maximum speed: 135 mph (217 km/h)

Range: 675 miles (1,086 km)

Armament: Two AGM-114 Hellfire missiles, four AIM-92 Stinger missiles, six AGM-176 Griffin air-to-surface missiles

The Predator tracked Omar as he left his bunker in a compound northwest of the city. As he traveled through the narrow and winding streets of Kandahar, it was difficult for the Predator to follow. Finally, the convoy parked at a compound just outside the city's outskirts.

The drone pilot, US Air Force captain Scott Swanson, expertly positioned the Predator to allow the sensor operator, Master Sergeant Scott Guay, to align and aim the Hellfire missiles. Captain Swanson held the Predator steady as Sergeant Guay pointed the laser designator on the truck and pulled the trigger. A plume of bright light flashed on the video screens, followed by a glow. The truck and several of the terrorists standing nearby had been detonated.

It was a historic moment for the Predator and a big leap forward in military warfare. That night, a distinctly new way of fighting was born.

A Day in the Life
of a Drone Pilot

Unlike traditional pilots who fly surveillance, fighter, or attack aircraft, drone pilots—or remotely piloted aircraft (RPA) pilots, as they prefer to be called—get to know their surveillance and strike targets well. Sitting at a computer console for eight hours at a time, air force pilots and their sensor operators conduct missions similar to a police stakeout, but thousands of miles away.

A typical drone combat air patrol (CAP) mission involves up to two hundred support personnel who provide mission intelligence information, aircraft and communications equipment maintenance, and aircraft launch and recovery. The drone captures live video of terrorist targets conducting daily business and interacting with their families and friends.

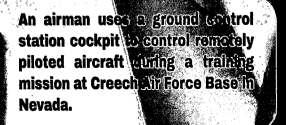

An airman uses a ground control station cockpit to control remotely piloted aircraft during a training mission at Creech Air Force Base in Nevada.

Can Drones Drive Business?

In December 2013, Amazon.com unveiled a project that it announced was the future of small-package delivery: drones. Amazon envisions a future where a small drone will pick up packages in small yellow buckets, whizzing them through the air to customers located within a ten-mile (16-km) radius only minutes after their online purchase is made. Amazon calls its "sky robot" the "octocopter," because it has eight rotors.

Amazon isn't the only company interested in drones as local consumer delivery vehicles. Domino's Pizza is testing a "Domicopter" to deliver pizzas in the United Kingdom. The health care industry is also interested in using drones to deliver blood and other lifesaving humanitarian aid to remote places inaccessible by ground vehicles, which could also help wounded ground troops get immediate medical supplies.

A quadcopter drone arrives with a small delivery at Deutsche Post headquarters in Germany. Deutsche Post was testing deliveries of medicine from a pharmacy.

Collecting Aerial Images After the Haiti Earthquake

In January 2010, a devastating earthquake struck Haiti, killing more than two hundred thousand people and destroying thousands of structures all over the island nation. Humanitarian agencies responded quickly, arriving to provide food, medical assistance, and temporary housing. But they didn't immediately know what areas were hit the hardest. The US Air Force redeployed Global Hawk drones to fly over the island, providing real-time images and video to emergency aid workers, enabling them to direct their supplies and personnel to the hardest-hit areas.

A Global Hawk drone

Like Lieutenant Colonel McCurley and his drone crew, these teams quietly watch their insurgent targets around the clock for months at a time, looking for changes in their daily patterns that might offer important intelligence information. It's a level of detail that traditional pilots never see from twenty thousand feet (6,096 m) above ground. So, when the call comes to make a strike against a target, the crew sees the consequences of their combat actions up close and personal.

What keeps them going? They get satisfaction when ground troops tell them that their intelligence and overhead surveillance saved American lives and kept them safe. Troops deployed far away from a base in Afghanistan are grateful that a drone is flying overhead, gathering important information. It allows them to get some much-needed rest, while the circling drone keeps a watchful eye on nearby insurgents.

So You Want to Be a Drone Pilot?

ccording to drone pilots, the toughest part about flying a UAV is that you can't feel what's going on. But the intensity of the flight and the importance of the drone missions make a career in this field of aviation increasingly attractive. Students are earning degrees in unmanned aircraft systems (UAS), the term used to describe the whole network of equipment necessary to support drones, including ground computers, software, and satellites. The University of North Dakota was the first university in the United States to offer a degree program in this field.

Initially offered in 2009 with five students enrolled, the program has rapidly increased in popularity as the job prospects in this category of aviation have exploded with opportunity. Some thirty schools now offer programs, including Embry-Riddle Aeronautical University in Arizona and Florida, and Kansas State University.

What Skills Do You Need to Be a Drone Pilot?

What skills does it take to become a drone pilot? You might think being a skilled video gamer is enough. Certainly, good hand-eye coordination is important. But knowledge of the STEM subjects— science, technology, engineering, and math—are critical to success. If you want to become a drone pilot, studying advanced math (calculus and statistics) and physics in high school or college will be helpful. In addition, the ability to endure long periods in front of computer screens is important, especially when coupled with strong concentration skills. The ability to pay attention to the fine details of complex maps and pictures is also very helpful. Finally, a curiosity about how machines and gadgets work will round out the skills you need to be a successful drone pilot.

A US Air Force pilot grasps a flight control and weapons firing stick while preparing to launch an MQ-1B Predator from a ground control station.

A computer display in a ground control station shows data as the crew of an MQ-9 Reaper flies a training mission.

While the number of traditional piloting jobs in the military and the commercial airline industry are decreasing, the need for drone pilots is expected to increase significantly.

Students first earn a commercial pilot certificate. Then, they learn about the components of unmanned aerial systems, including drone cameras, ground systems, and communications platforms. Then, they spend up to seventy hours in a drone simulator. Finally, they learn about the fast-changing laws surrounding military and commercial drone usage. Air force drone crews receive an additional year of training before flying operational missions.

The Future

As computer technology became more and more advanced and computer devices became smaller and smaller, it was not long before engineers envisioned even tinier drones. Micro aerial vehicles (MAVs) are miniature drones and are often as small as a hummingbird or a bumblebee. They are used for government, commercial, research, or military purposes.

Some of these MAVs are incorporating bird-like features such as flapping wings or pinching claws that can grasp or perch on a surface. This will be handy for both military and humanitarian use.

Maritime Drones: The Future of the Navy?

Navy submarines use a variety of tactics to evade detection and operate in enemy waters to collect intelligence, insert Navy SEALs for counterterrorism missions, and launch missiles. Submarine crews do this very quietly so their location is not discovered. Submarines and their crews are known as the "silent service." Between 360–560 feet (109.7–170.6 m) in length, these vessels and their large crews can be easily found by enemy radar and sonar. Now imagine how hard it would be for the nation's enemies to detect a five-foot-long (1.5 m) unmanned submarine. There are also drones that can operate without any interaction with a human crew at all—like a robot—providing information about undersea activities.

The US Navy is now testing various unmanned underwater vehicle (UUV) designs to perform a variety of missions, including reconnaissance, mine detection, and search and salvage. The navy recently completed tests on the GhostSwimmer UUV, which is

FACT

Drones and the Law

In 2011, a drone strike killed known Al Qaeda terrorist Anwar al-Awlaki in Yemen. However, he was an American, a Muslim who became radicalized. Though he had become an enemy combatant, US law prohibits killing an American citizen without a trial. Drone warfare had just entered a gray area of the law. Was he killed illegally or was his assassination justified by a 2001 congressional law, the Authorization to Use Military Force (AUFM), which gave the United States the authority to use lethal force abroad against enemy combatants—even against its own citizens?

The GhostSwimmer is cleverly crafted to have the look and swimming style of a large fish.

approximately five feet (1.5 m) long and weighs one hundred pounds (45 kg). It can operate in water depths ranging from 10 inches (25 cm) to 300 feet (91 m). It can either work independently using a battery, or it can be controlled via laptop with a 500-foot (152-m) tether, providing instantaneous data to the laptop. It mimics the shape and swimming style of a large fish, including an oscillating tail fin!

The Submarine Rescue Diving and Recompression System (SRDRS) is an underwater drone that can rapidly respond to a damaged submarine trapped underwater. It can attach itself to the submarine at depths of two thousand feet (610 m) to rescue and provide assistance to trapped crew members.

A US Army lieutenant prepares to launch a Puma drone. The small drone can be tossed into the air by one person.

Coast Guard Drones: Operation Deep Freeze

At the US Coast Guard's remote Antarctica outpost, McMurdo Station, the service and a number of other government agencies perform Arctic research. In 2016, the coast guard brought the Puma AE "All Environment" drone to assist in icebreaking efforts. This drone, which weighs 13.5 pounds (6 kg) and can fly for more than 210 minutes, has a range of nine miles (14.48 km) and can stream live video back to the ground control station. It can be hand tossed, sent out ahead of a Coast Guard icebreaker to scout the icy waters of Antarctica for the best possible route. It can land on the ground or on the water. It literally gives a coast guard crew a bird's-eye view of their path through dangerous waters.

Drones are here to stay. They are much less expensive than conventional aircraft and safer for the crew because they are operated remotely. Many military analysts actually believe they will eventually replace all manned aircraft. Indeed, some military leaders have said that the military's newest jet, the F-22 Raptor stealth fighter, might just be the last piloted aircraft the military builds.

1806—The Royal Navy launches kites over the coast of France.

1849—Austrians launch armed balloons over the city of Venice.

1863—Union and Confederate forces test out Charles Perley's aerial bomber, a hot air balloon laden with explosives.

1898—Corporal William Eddy uses a drone to obtain aerial surveillance photos during the Spanish-American War.

1910—General Motors engineer Charles Kettering invents the Kettering Aerial Torpedo.

1913—Dr. Peter Hewitt and Elmer A. Sperry introduce the Sperry Aerial Torpedo during World War I.

1935—Designed by the UK as an aerial target, the radio-controlled Queen Bee drone is used as target practice.

1944—The US Navy develops Operation Aphrodite during World War II, a program using UAVs that are initially manned by a two-man crew and are then vacated and flown as bombs.

1960s—The US Air Force develops combat UAV called the AQM-34 Ryan Firebee, which is air-launched from a DC-130 aircraft, dropped with a parachute, and recovered with a helicopter.

1995—Defense contractor designs the "Gnat," or the RQ-1 Predator, a remotely piloted glider with a video camera.

2001—The first weaponized Predator, equipped with Hellfire missiles, is deployed to Afghanistan.

2009—University of North Dakota becomes the first university to offer a degree in unmanned aircraft systems.

2011—American Al Qaeda terrorist Anwar al-Awlaki is killed by a drone strike in Yemen.

Al Qaeda—A radical Islamic group organized by Osama bin Laden in the 1990s to engage in terrorist activities.

CAP mission—A type of flying mission for fighter and drone aircraft. Also called a combat air patrol mission.

drone—The term commonly used to describe unmanned aerial vehicles.

Global Positioning System (GPS)—A radio navigation system that uses multiple satellites to allow land, sea, and airborne users to determine their exact location, velocity, and time anywhere on earth.

ground control station (GCS)—The computer equipment and software on the ground that receives video and sensor data from an airborne drone and can transmit commands back to the drone.

Hellfire missile—An air-to-surface missile first developed for anti-armor use. Also called the heliborne-launched, fire-and-forget missile.

micro aerial vehicle (MAV)—A very small UAV; some are as small as a bird or an insect.

military intelligence—A discipline that uses information collection and analysis techniques that provides guidance and direction to the military in support of their decisions.

military surveillance—Close observation of the battle area for the purpose of providing timely information and combat intelligence.

remotely piloted aircraft (RPA)/remotely piloted vehicle (RPV)—More formal terms for drones.

satellite—An artificial body placed in orbit around the earth or moon or another planet in order to collect information or for communication.

sortie—An operation flight by a single aircraft.

unmanned aerial vehicle (UAV)—A formal term for drones. The military frequently calls them unmanned aerial systems (UAS) to reflect the fact that the drones operate with a ground and satellite communications system.

unmanned underwater vehicle (UUV)—A drone that operates underwater, usually under the ocean.

BOOKS

Baichtal, John. *Building Your Own Drones: A Beginners' Guide to Drones, UAVs, and ROVs.* Indianapolis, IN: Que Publishing, 2015.

LaFay, Mark. *Drones for Dummies.* Hoboken, NJ: John Wiley and Sons, Inc., 2015.

McCurley, T. Mark. *Hunter Killer: Inside America's Unmanned Air War.* New York: Dutton Publishing, 2015.

Whittle, Richard. *Predator: The Secret Origins of the Drone Revolution.* New York: Henry Holt and Company, 2014.

WEBSITES

Air Force

www.airforce.com

Read more about careers in the US Air Force and how you can become a drone pilot in the military.

Smithsonian National Air and Space Museum

airandspace.si.edu

Learn about the history of aviation and space exploration at the Smithsonian Institute's National Air and Space Museum in Washington, DC.

University of North Dakota Department of Aviation

aviation.und.edu

Learn how to become a civilian drone pilot with a UAS degree from the University of North Dakota.

INDEX

A
Al Qaeda, 4, 24, 41
Authorization to Use
    Military Force (AUFM),
    41

B
balloon bombs, 13, 15
bin Laden, Osama, 4-5,
    24, 26-27
Bosnia, 19, 23-24
Bush, George, 27

C
Central Intellience
    Agency (CIA), 16-17,
    23-24, 26-27
Civil War, 13
combat air patrol (CAP),
    31

D
drone pilots, 5, 8, 30, 31,
    35, 36-37, 39
    education for, 36-37, 39
    skills of, 37
drones
    aerial images, 16-17, 34
    business and, 33
    law and, 39, 41
    missile strikes, 8
    video surveillance,
    17, 19

F
flying bombs, 13, 15-16

G
global positioning
    system (GPS), 19
Gulf War, 27

H
Haiti earthquake, 34
Hellfire missile, 18, 27,
    30
Hewitt-Sperry Automatic
    Airplane, 13

I
Israeli Air Force, 21-22

M
McCurley, T. Mark, 4-8,
    10, 35
micro aerial vehicles
    (MAVs), 40
missiles, 8, 18, 22, 27,
    29-30, 40

O
Omar, Mullah
    Mohammed, 27, 30
Operation Aphrodite,
    15-16
Operation Deep Freeze,
    43-44

P
Perley, Charles, 13
Predator, 6-7, 10, 17,
    19, 20, 22-24, 26-27,
    29-30, 37

R
Reaper, 20
remotely piloted aircraft
    (RPA), 31
Royal Air Force, 15
Royal Navy, 11

S
sensor operator, 9, 30, 31
silent service, 40-41
Soviet Union, 16, 24
Submarine Rescue
    Diving and
    Recompression
    System (SRDRS), 43

T
terrorists, 4-6, 10, 24, 27,
    30, 31, 41

U
unmanned aerial vehicle
    (UAV), 16-17, 36
unmanned aircraft
    systems (UAS), 36
unmanned underwater
    vehicle (UUV), 41-42
US Air Force, 4-5, 8, 16,
    24, 30, 31, 34, 39
US Coast Guard, 43-44
US Navy, 13, 41-42

W
World War I, 13, 15
World War II, 15-16